ACADIANA

ACADIANA

NANCY REDDY

Black
Lawrence
Press

Black
Lawrence
Press

www.blacklawrence.com

Executive Editor: Diane Goettel
Chapbook Editor: Kit Frick
Book and Cover Design: Amy Freels
Cover art: "Untitled" (2014) by Lise Latreille. Used with permission.

Published 2018 by Black Lawrence Press.
Printed in the United States.

Contents

Dirge

First the sky
broken by birds

flying at the wrong season.
Then the heat goes and the breath goes out

and we are left alone and voiceless

between the blue untextured sky
and the terrible smooth water.

And then the howling like the seam ripped out
and all the under waters and the roaring gods.

After, the live oaks and honey locusts storm-shorn.
The shorebirds' great nests splintered
and all the fishing houses split-legged and sodden.

After, the dead lifted in their rotten boxes
and left to bob in storm water. The shoreline
carried out to sea.

What is this raw and wind-worn place
we have survived into. The wrong gods

roar into our lungs now.
A weeping sound like that. Like those birds

calling across the suddenly open water.

Girl Chooses Flight

She bought a black dog
because she wanted bad luck. She drove south
as far as the dark mood would move her.

And on the radio—nothing but Christ and zydeco:

Once in heaven—once in hell—
you don't get to come back and try it over.
You don't get to call back Lazarus.

She drove long hours through the parched towns
and two-pump truck stops of the northern parishes,
the highway striped with blown-out tires,
her hood and windshield black with love bugs
locked in mating.

And then the swamp before her
like a ballroom with the lid torn off.

The air at that first hour
had the sheen and hue of polished silver.
Slender tree trunks, weathered gray and splintered,
poked through still water.

A voice said *stay*. She stayed.

•

The girl seemed to stay like that for days, a fixed star
in the emergency pull-off lane.

At night the black dog blanketed her and at dawn
they pressed their faces to the glass. Hard to say
what she thought of then. Or what she waited for.

Then the god appeared to her in denim.
He asked her for one kiss and when she dodged

he spit into her mouth.

After that, the girl's hair grew golden
and sticky as corn silk. After that
the girl spoke only lies.

The Sibyls Choose Her

She had the sun-split look
of one whom the god has loved, however briefly

and she was weeping and speechless
when we pulled her from the car. No longer fit
for life in town.

We carried her to the swamp bed
and laid her by the fire. Her hair smelled then
of lemongrass and dishwater.

We used slivered sedge for kindling
and sliced the shorebird down its spine.

We bled the bird into the marsh
and when the water did not hiss and blacken
we knew the girl would do.

We pulled the dark meat from the ribs
and fed it to the sleeping girl.

When the girl was full and cradled
we let the flames die down and held her
to the fire's former heart

and seared her tongue against the rocks to bridle it.
A terrible and unhinged shrieking. Then

she opened her throat
and sang.

Saint Charlene Offers Up Her Suffering

O Lord, bless
if you can find it in your heart

the vowel. It moves,
an aspirant between my teeth,

it makes possible the consonants
that build our petaled world. It is

a meager thing, the vowel. Lord,
I have been prayed over

twice today, have heard my given name
spoken to you by men I barely know.

I cannot tell if you are listening.
Should I have felt

some movement in the trees,
Lord? The magnolia blossoms

already a wilted mass on the lawn.
I cannot answer you

without the paper vowels,
each open sound a blossom. I cannot

hear you for the breeze.

The Thibodeaux Girls

The girls wanted heat on them.

Nights they snuck off the sleeping porch,
their hair wild with humidity, their legs
downy and freckled. Their tongues

still sweet from cow corn
they'd stripped from the far field after dinner.

One-handed, they lifted their nightdresses above their heads
and swung them across the clothesline by the quilts.

The white cloth flapped and the girls lay naked,
the dewy lawn blading them,
as they dared themselves to stay

still as Sunday dinner. Some nights
the kittens followed and curled
their soft and fine-boned bodies

against the sisters' girlish aches and peaks. One girl
grew faster than the others and wore her hair
in a braid that bounced against her spine.

When her blood first came
she slept the way her mother taught her,

curtains drawn and swamp teeth beneath her pillow.

She dreamed her one true love and saw him
only from the back.

The First Miracle

After sunrise service papa walked us to the marsh's edge
     and as we raised our palms up to the pinking skyline,
one by one he lit a box of barnburners and held each glowing tip
     against the thin web of skin beside my thumb
and while the little ones looked on, he peeled the blister back
     to show the new skin risen opalescent beneath my worldly
flesh. Papa breathed a wish into my palm and the wound bloomed
     a cloud of honeysuckle. The sweet scent made me sick
and mama called us all to come inside, to change and
     start our chores. *Tell no one*, papa said.

Signs Resembling Sacraments

When the rooster won't rise
        and the loaves won't sing, find the girl
and carry her to the river

        Hold her under
until her hair fans
        the riverbed's darkest smoothest rocks,
until her eyes loll in their sockets
                then snap open. The air is so still
that her eyelashes flapping
        ripple the water's slippery top.

We do not know precisely
        the nature of this sin's
transmission, only that
        a tongue once split
will not flare up again
                in flame and speech.

        So hold her
longer. Her nightdress is a puff of smoke.
        The water cools and calms her.

If she rises now, her ribcage will be a tinderbox,
        all spark and ash. So let the river
have her. The current will carry her
        to where the river opens
its mouth to the sea.

In a hurricane-blue sky

a young pilot tests bombs
over a field of canvas. The season

has been a quiet one; the canvas shreds
like wheat. The field

rips open like a woman's dress.
Afterward, streaks of color, shattered.

In the field below

so small she almost
is not there

a woman plays the frayed fabric
like a harp. The pilot thinks
of the girl at home, the picture he sent

of himself masked in the cockpit. He wonders
that it is possible to think of this—
a woman's eyes, her breasts,

even now, flying above this field
pocked by detonation. Even now he

feels her heart drying to a single sheet of plaster.

The woman in the field is playing,
though the notes have all been swallowed now.

She wants to name that sound, the space of
after. It is like hearing
on the radio the voice of a man

who has recently died. It is like the whistling
of a room emptied for the last time.

And all this time, the field ululating
like a canyon or a boneyard.

Asterope in Grand Isle

In the scraped-belly field, a woman in a white dress. Or a woman wishing
for a white dress. She wished for clarity or at least a sky cleared

of aircraft. She wished a sky in which nothing moved. She didn't want
to be seen like that, her head exposed from the air like a cracked plate.

All the birds above were full of men whose hands
she'd never know whose eyes stripped the color from her hair: a flock

of eyes. She wished them all still and silent wished their whirring
engines to a stop and when she'd wished she heard the sky go silent.

She wished the skies flightless and she grounded all the winged birds
like that, wishing. Grounded, their hands were cold and thin

like tissues or twigs. She could walk anywhere now. The field
this late in the year grown tan and crisp with unharvested crops.

Wildflowers wintering along the fence posts. She wanted to be the only
body moving so she wished the heartbeats still. A hush fell.

Saint James at the Ascension Parish Drive-In

By ten the gravel lot was throbbing
with the exposition of a double feature's
second half. I saw the girl asleep
beside an idling Buick, her arms thrown
into the wheel well as if embracing
the still-warm rubber or the axle.
Her shocked-blonde hair a fallow field
against the rusted panel. We do not know
how to pray as we ought. Every woman
in this town is stuffed with sin, teetering
in heels. When I got close I saw I knew
the sleeping girl. Her wicked sisters
giggled and posed along the fence, side-eying
the boys sitting in a borrowed truck bed.
Because her mother knew she'd be her last
and was yet another girl born wailing,
her hair even in that first-breath moment
a slick curl above her labor-flattened skull,
she named her for her sorrows.
Her eyes not yet turned dark, they christened her
Dolores and were done. I sat beside her
on the gravel-studded crabgrass
and held my hand above her mouth
to feel her hot breath on my palm.
Each exhalation's puff of sticky air parted
her lips briefly, revealing a lost baby tooth's
pink root. Once her tongue flicked against it

as if the spot were sore. I wanted then
to cup my palms and lower them against
her lips and throat to feel her body
shudder as she gasped and woke. The moment
passed. I touched only the soft and untanned
arch of one sandaled foot. The drive-in's climax
of explosions and gunfire threw our silhouettes
into relief against the field behind us.
When I left her she was still unharmed.

Holy Week, Acadiana

One whole holy week no air moved in town.

The ladies brought their boys to kneel
and fan them. We lit votives for the four men
lost out on a deep sea rig
and watched the flames inside the airless chapel,
still as stained-glass saints. They wavered only

when the congregation stood or kneeled,
when we sang in unison
the gospel's final *hallelujah*. Hard to know,

that long hot week of noon mass, the hours
at the stations and the passion, how to pray.

The oilmen brought back three bodies
and the lost man's wife swore
he was out there somewhere breathing, still.

So if you wished the lost man risen,
where was he? And what would he have seen?

As in storm season: if you prayed for mercy
or wished away a strong storm's landfall,
weren't you also wishing harm

on someone else's town?
One rule was:
you couldn't wish away the sorrow
the Lord saw fit to grant you

because even sorrow was firm proof of His hand.
I folded my head against my folded knuckles and whispered
the only sure safe words I knew:
please, Lord. Please.

All at once the air became
a fist. Then it was a palm.
It slapped me down.

And when I rose I was wailing
and speaking. The Lord a light
inside my ribcage. My tongue
a tongue of fire. At the wrong season.
The women called
for cool damp cloths. The priest was wearing
the wrong shade robe for prophecy.
The men quieted and carried me

out the wide church doors, lifting
by the ankles and the shoulders.
They laid me out.

Town Anatomy II

[*the Sibyls speak*]
Our tongues are marvelous,
all fire and revelation.

The men come
dirty-haired and swamp-eyed.

They kneel. We make them.

And when the spirit comes
we speak. When the spirit comes

we are roaring and plate-eyed.

It is like cicadas
like a seawall
in the skull.

Not your indoor god, all candles
and low hum. Though the men

come not for answers, but to hear
their words reflected
in a woman's pitch.

The girls come only
when they are swelled up

and the trouble is on them heavy.

Sometimes we let them sit
the heavy months with us.

Sometimes we take the trouble
mewling from their breasts
and kiss the trouble

so it will learn to sing. Sometimes
we leave it wailing below the cypress

and watch the hawks swoop down.

Saint Catherine Takes the Auspices

We're out back in our lawn chairs under the carport
when the air drops and thins as before the storm
that's said will break us. We divide the sky

into four regions and watch for signs.
As the red dog's fur sends smoke skyward
to whatever gods may still watch over us,

I sprinkle holy water along the fence posts, place
the blessed palms along the shuttered windows
and above the doorframes. I make of matches a cross

and light them quick to stop the rain.
The sky's a still and cloudless blue
and tells us nothing. Only certain birds

can guide us. They do not appear.

Storm Pastoral

On the last day   the radio reports a deer   how it walked
on neutral ground on sidewalks   through gardens through

Audubon Park but how   did it get here   this city of water
city like a teacup   a cupped palm in the Gulf

the Mississippi and Lake Ponchartrain   the twinspan
the causeway and I-10 over swamps   the only way out

this swishing thickness   the sound of water   in the body
of weather in the bones   like those men in the South Pacific

who survived shipwreck   sharks the screams   of other men
rescue   and when the hands descended   from the rescue boats

the men's skin was waterlogged   and peeled off in sheets.

The Thibodeaux Girl Speaks, After

We wake to a world
shaken out of square.

Tree limbs spike the lawn.
The live oaks are upended
and roots the size of a sedan
face sunward.

Every stoplight in town
is dark and the sidewalks
are slick with shucked leaves.

The creeks and bayous
are storm-swollen.
Shimmering runoff
bloats their banks.

Before the axes and the chainsaws
and the children carrying
what small limbs they can,
an after-storm stillness

so the whole town
speaks like church.

And in the swamp outside town,
a stand of bald cypress
is gaunt and silvered
in the brackish water.

Hawks call for prey
from their perches
at the marsh's edge.

Saltwater and subsidence
etch a dark path
through the swamp.

The stories say
the river held us
in its mouth.

Then the river
shifted west again
and we were left
dry-boned and sorrowful.

We live now in later times,
with levees and spillways that hold the river
to its shores, with waters
rising yearly in the gulf.

Now is when we'd like to pray
but we've forgotten all the words.

The Sibyls Swear Away Their Prophecy

Do not come here
asking why your crops are taken by the waters
why the oyster beds are wind-wracked and scattered.

Go ask your robed men who teach the split-world after
who read by rote that thin-skinned book of mercy and ruin

why this country is unseamed and stripped.

What else is this but vengeance. As the gods
would will it. As in the last hour.

You should give thanks for the brutal water
the days of sun without cease the weather
that grants the hardship that shapes your days.

You ask small questions and for this you will not be forgiven.

Fog Dancing

And when the low planes came
        to spray for mosquitoes,
the townspeople danced in the fog,

        green and gauzy as it was,
and when the babies grew crooked and raw-spined,
        they didn't know

which gods to blame,
        the white-walled Christ of town
or the wild-haired gods of the swamp.

The Siren of Barataria

As a baby she was given to the swamp.

      She was laid down in the reeds
and swaddled in the maiden cane still summer-bright.
She cried one time and the boatman came running.

He laid a dew-slick strip of swamp grass
on her tongue and when she swallowed it was sweet

and struck her dumb.

      So it was not her voice
that called the waters from the gulf.
She never wished the winds, the cracking and the weeping
and the wailing sounds that came from town.

The god found her as she slept below the overpass.
He stitched a feather collar along her clavicle

and so gave her back her voice. After that
she was a songbird.

They went on this way some time, singing and touching
as the waters rose and receded.

Then, after several seasons' calm,
the god found a farmhand whose ankle he longed to kiss.
The siren smelled the barnyard on him
and she knew.

When the townsmen came to flush the winter game
with burning, the siren walked a slow loop in the lit grass.
The whole marsh smoked with smoldering peat.
Her white dress caught and turned to ash.

Following a Long Illness, Saint Bernardine Confesses

When they found him in his wildness, in the wilderness
of swamp and sky and sea receding, when they found him
unwashed and ragged, when they saw his skin like wax,
the skeleton of him, the jagged voice of no companionship,
when they saw the stars, the constellations wrong so far from town,
when he refused to stand or even answer—
they carried him, and for a long time he could not speak
but simply rustled and wept into the horsehair mattress
and then, after a time, he was born again
again, the tongues and fire, the women waiting
for him to rise and tell them what he'd seen.
　　　　Before she died the child-saint
was wearing red pajamas. When we found him
he was holding the scraps of crimson flannel to his face.
The saint says he placed the consecrated host
beneath the child's tongue to ease her journey.
He says his hands will heal us
though the healing may not reach us in this life.

After, the Sibyls Fall Out of Words

No god moves us now

so we are wordless and unhinged,
like the dark-ribbed maidens
lost to the gulf. We won't have

the men's hands on us now. Not even
the god like a horsemaster.
He's just a whisper in the under

now. When the rain comes
we open our throats to it.
When the storms come
we are crucified to the pylons.

Saved and spared are different
and you will learn that now.

Acknowledgments

Grateful acknowledgment to the editors of the following journals, where poems from this collection first appeared, sometimes in slightly different form.

32 Poems: "The Thibodeaux Girls"

A Poetry Congeries, Connotation Press: "Dirge," "The Siren of Barataria," "Town Anatomy II," and "After, the Sibyls Run out of Words"

Connotation Press: "Girl Chooses Flight" and "Signs Resembling Sacraments"

Crab Orchard Review: "Holy Week, Acadiana"

Jabberwock Review: "Saint Charlene Offers Up Her Suffering" (as "Devotional")

Radar Poetry: "The Sibyls Swear Away Their Prophecy," "The Thibodeaux Girl Speaks, After," "St. James at the Ascension Parish Drive-In," and "The Sibyls Choose Her"

Raleigh Review: "The First Miracle"

This project had its beginnings in a summer of writing in a tiny, cob-webby carrel in Memorial Library at the University of Wisconsin-Madison. I am thankful for the support of the Dorothy D. Bailey Summer Prize Scholarship from Wisconsin's MFA program, which funded that time.

Before that, these poems were shaped by my life in New Orleans before and just after Hurricane Katrina, and they are written with love and the greatest admiration for the joy and resilience of the people of the Gulf Coast. These poems are animated—I hope—by the exuberance and brilliance of my first students, the ninth graders at Marion Abramson Senior High School in New Orleans East.

The opening narrative of "Holy Week, Acadiana" owes a debt to Kelli Charles. Gay M. Gomez's *The Louisiana Coast: Guide to an American Wetland* (Texas A & M UP, 2008) was an invaluable aid in the early drafting of these poems.

I'd like to extend my particular thanks to Rachel Marie Patterson and Dara-Lyn Shrager, editors of *Radar Poetry*, whose selection of several of these poems as finalists for the 2016 Coniston Prize encouraged me to send this project out as a collection.

Many thanks to the editorial team at Black Lawrence, especially Kit Frick, who've made such a good home for these poems. With grati-tude to my poetry teachers and to my MFA cohort, who were the first readers for many of these poems. With appreciation for my colleagues in the writing program at Stockton University. And for Smith, my love and my partner.